focus on

Holywell-cum-Needingworth

images of a village

About the author

The Author
(Photograph: Brian Jones)

Joe Newell was born in 1921 and lived for the first 14 years of his life at Manor Farm, Holywell, which was at that time a mixed arable/dairy farm struggling through the agricultural depression of the pre-war years. His schooling at St Ives Grammar School he sees as secondary to his life on the farm, where he learnt an abiding love of the countryside, its pursuits and a respect for those who earn their living working the land – our most precious heritage.

Joe still regards Holywell as his natural home although he now lives in retirement in St Ives.

By the same author:
The Holywell Story (1991)
Holywell and Needingworth (1999)

focus on

Holywell-cum-Needingworth

images of a village

Joe Newell

First published 2005

ISBN 0-9550719-0-9

Published by
Flagholme Press
Hawthorn Cottage
Back Lane
Holywell
Cambridgeshire PE27 5JP

Typeset in 11/12pt Verdana and Bernhard Roman Modern
Printed and made in Great Britain by Blackwell John Buckle, Great Yarmouth, Norfolk

Contents

The Manor House, Holywell, c.1900

Acknowledgements

Without the enthusiastic help of many people it would have been impossible to produce this book. People have gone through their personal collections and searched in lumber rooms and attics for that elusive photograph which was known to be somewhere. I have been a privileged 'gatherer' and have learned much about Holywell and Needingworth in the process.

In particular my thanks are due to the following people:

Jack Arnold
Wilf Asplin
Pauline and John Baily
George Britton
Tristan De Vere Cole
J. Di Inorio
Brigid Elsdon
Eileen Gray
Jill Harvey
Evelyn Henson
Christine Johnson

Joan Jordan
Mabel Lantaff
Alan Mott
Clare Palmer-Asplin
Tim Pearce-Higgins
Marion Pratt
Ken Sandifer
Charlie Stocker
Sid Tabbitt
Graham Whitfield

In addition, my thanks also go to June York, for her interest and skill with which she has turned my complicated manuscript into an attractive book, and to the Cambridge Collection, Cambridge Newspapers Ltd, the County Records Office, the Norris Museum Library and the Parish Council.

Church Street, Needingworth, opposite Park View

There are other places
Which are the world's end,
Some at the sea's jaws,
Or over a dark lake, in a desert or a city -
But this is the nearest, in place and time,
Now and in England
                                    T. S. Eliot

From a watercolour by Robert Winter. Sothebys, London

High Street, Needingworth 1898

The Parish Church of
St John the Baptist
Holywell-cum-Needingworth

In the year 969 Oswald, Archbishop of York, with Ailwyn, Alderman of all England, founded the convent of Ramsey for a body of Benedictine monks. The endowment of the monastery included Haliewell, given by Alfwara a 'noble Saxon lady'.

In the year 990 Gode was sent by Ramsey to Holywell and is the first recorded priest, although it may be assumed that a holy place or cell was in existence before he arrived. A memorial to the fallen of both world wars is in the south aisle of the church. The brass cross and candlesticks were given by Mrs A. A. Fraser in memory of her son Alistair.

The eagle lectern was given by Reginald Mortimer to commemorate the Diamond Jubilee of Queen Victoria

In 1845 the basin of the well was restored and surrounded by a brick canopy. A brass plate bears the inscription 'Erected by the Rev S. B. Beckwith, Rector of this parish A.D. 1845'.

The Patronal Festival and village feast commences on the first Sunday after 24th June. Dressing the well is now an established feature of the Patronal Festival and was introduced in 1980 by the Rev Joe Wilcox, who came from Derbyshire where the art is widely practised.

Interior view of carved oak chancel screen from the nave

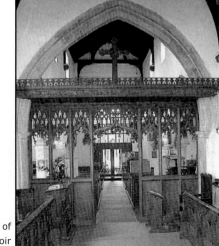

Interior view of screen from the choir

For many years the biblical pictures, created from petals and leaves, etc. was the work of the local Horticultural Society. More recently it is the creation of enthusiastic parishioners.

The 'Holy Well'

Rev Joe Wilcox. Rector 1980–1986

Some recent examples of the well dressing

The new design, introduced in 2004

Rev Pearce-Higgins MA
Rector of Holywell-cum-
Needingworth 1946–1960

Remembrance Day Parade 2004

The Rev Owen Swan, Rector of Holywell-cum-
Needingworth (1987-1998) offers celebratory gifts to the
Right Honourable John Major MP, Chancellor of the
Exchequer, at the Millennium Fete on 23rd June 1990

The Rev Elizabeth Strickland receives a cheque for
£400 for the Restoration Fund from Rose Killock,
President of the Over-60s Club.

Holywell Front

Haymaking (the old way) in Church Hole c.1909 From a water-colour by Robert Winter (another of similar date by Sutton Palmer)

Haymaking (the new way) in Church Hole 2004 by Farmer James Anderson

A Massey-Harris hayloader at work in Flaggholme 1930

'Goodyers' purchased in 1924 by Gerald and Madge Baily for £124 (originally two cottages)

Robert Winter lived most of his life in Holywell and is seen here busy at his easel on Holywell Front

Spring Cottage, the home of Robert James Winchester Fraser (1872-1930), who signed his paintings Robert Winter to distinguish himself from his father

The village postbox was in the wall, until the wall collapsed. Now it really is a 'post' box

Hill Farm, dated 1623 on the chimney, was the 1930s home of the West family, poultry farmers from Lancashire.

(Various photographs of farm activity)

The common land, banks and verges of the parish were let by the parish council to dairymen who had a few cows but little pasture. Dorothy Ibbett was a cow girl and is shown here 'minding' her charges

Godfrey the baker along Holywell Front

Cattle grazing on common land by Berrie House. The name of the minder is not known

Oak Cottage to the left
of the picture and next
door the tiny cottage
now called 'The
Quarterdeck', c.1903

Norah Tabbitt c.1925, with
hoop - later to become a
teacher at Holywell School

David and Norah Tabbitt lived at Oak
Cottage with their six sons (left to
right, top row: Walter, Sid, Eric;
below: baby Stanley, Frank and Reg)
and daughter Norah

Seasonal boat repair 1950

Ferryboat in foreground. *Left to right*: Brooklyn, The Anchor Public House and Reed Cottage

G. B. Fraser in the garden of Reed Cottage with Mary his daughter (1899-1921)

Reed Cottage (right), home of artist Gilbert Baird Fraser (1866-1947). His wife May (Heseltine) ran a small fee-paying school from the cottage 1934

Flood water 1921, looking East

Flood water 1921, looking West. The waters of the River Great Ouse rose to flood level several times each year, often reaching the footpath

Tom Arnold cutting the rush harvest

Dolly Arnold with Kitty, her pony

Tom Arnold laying an eel trap

The Ferry Boat

In the nineteenth century there was wharfage at Holywell for coal and other goods brought up the river by barge. There was a brick and tile works behind the inn and hovels for the workers. The clay pit has only recently been filled in to become the Ferryboat car park.

An 1890 photograph of 'The Boat' Inn

The Ferryboat 1909 from a water colour by Robert Winter

The sign as it is today

The cottage to the left of the inn is now part of the whole

The inn enjoyed a few years as 'Ye Olde Ferryboat Inn' (as shown on the sign)

The artist W. F. Garden (1856-1921) resided at the Ferryboat - fell down the steps, fractured his skull and died. Beware!

Another painting of the Ferryboat by W. F. Garden

An early photograph
of the Ferry Boat

The Floodbank pictured in May - one mile to
the Pike and Eel

'Wildcroft', home of the Metcalf family with the distant Ferryboat

56570. Holywell Village; St. Ives, Hunts.

Wildcroft showing Tom Metcalf's accessory shop for fishermen. Maggots etc. always available!

The Ferry Boat Inn
2005

Back Lane, Holywell & Manor Farm

Briar Cottage, Back Lane, Holywell
Bought at auction for £130 by Mary Willmer and her
home until she died in her 100th year in 1991

The House of Dreams, so named by Joan
Greathead because she found happiness
there

Tom Metcalf, Wildfowler/ Fisherman A countryman of many talents, at the door of the White Horse

The White Horse Public House 1910
Godfrey, the Needingworth baker, delivering in his dog cart

The White Horse looking west and next to it Croft Cottages. Next to the pub lived Bertha Lily Day (1870-1959), a retired schoolmistress. She once had a Tabbitt boy removed from church service for fidgeting (tapping his foot on the pew woodwork)

White Rose Cottage
Home of Arthur Anderson Fraser, artist
(1861-1904). Founder member of the
White Cockade Jacobite Club c.1890

The Manor, Holywell
On July 15th, 1888, a severe electrical storm struck and felled a Lombardy Poplar which caused damage to the front of the house and broke some 70 panes of glass in the windows

Top the house before restoration
Left after restoration

Sanders Spencer (1840-1930) Came to Holywell in 1875, a pioneer breeder of Yorkshire and Middle White pigs. Over the next 40 years his pigs were exported to 45 countries and won more than 2500 prizes at agricultural shows

Middle White Boar 'Holywell Rosador'. The breed was ideal for large Victorian families but is now classified as a rare breed and can only be seen at such places as the National Trust's Wimpole Hall

Middle White Sow 'Holywell Perfection'. Mr Spencer said of his pigs 'the sows are excellent mothers, gentle with their young, and permitting the attendant to handle them at will, even to the extent of examining their teeth!'

Mrs Spencer established the 'St Oswald's apiary' in the Manor gardens - named in honour of Oswald who purchased the Manorial rights of Holywell from King Edward in the 10th century

Mrs Charles Spencer with her daughters Nancy and Katherine, about to set out visiting in their donkey cart

Sanders Spencer also bred dairy shorthorn cattle and his successor, William H. Newell, is shown here with 'Cornerstone', a prize shorthorn bull

Fred and Amelia Tabbit with daughter Mary. Fred was herdsman to the Holywell pigs. An acknowledged expert on the breeding programme, Fred travelled Europe with stock, yet he had no formal education

The Manor Farm sale catalogue 1935

27th March, 1935.   Without Reserve.

THE MANOR FARM, HOLYWELL,
NEAR ST. IVES. HUNTS.

Catalogue of Unreserved Dispersal Sale of the whole of the Live and Dead

FARM STOCK
including

THE HERD OF
36 DAIRY COWS & HEIFERS
Bull and 14 Head of Young Stock

10 HORSES

3 Sows and Litters, 40 Strong Store Pigs,
POULTRY AND 5 GEESE,

THE IMPLEMENTS, MACHINES,
Carts, Harness, Barn Tackle, Poultry Houses,
Dairy Utensils and other Effects

WHICH

MR. CYRIL WATTS

Has been instructed by MRS. NEWELL (who has sold the Farm), to Sell by Auction, on

WEDNESDAY, 27th MARCH, 1935
Commencing at 11 o'clock prompt.

Refreshments will be provided.

Catalogues may be obtained of the Auctioneer, St. Ives.
Telephone No. 11.

DARLOW, PRINTER, FREE CHURCH PASSAGE, ST. IVES.

Topping out W. H. Newell, Bill Leach, John Coulson

The last load of harvest. Henry Newell on the cart. 'Boxer' between the shafts

Harvest 1930 Bill Leach, pigman
with 'Smart', a young gelding.
Bill's hand is on Smart's nose to
prevent him shying at the camera

Tom Paisley 1947 - post-war owner of Manor Farm. A steam and traction engine
enthusiast. Two views of his engine sheds

Eventide view of the farm

THE IMPORTANT & HISTORIC

PAISLEY COLLECTION

STEAM TRACTION ENGINES
LOCOMOTIVE & TRACTION PLATES
AND ANCILLARY EQUIPMENT & EFFECTS
(420 LOTS)

E EKINS, DILLEY & HANDLEY
Centenary House, Huntingdon, Cambridgeshire
Tel. Huntingdon (0480) 56171

Catalogue £2 (to admit 2 persons)

By direction of the Personal Representatives of the
late T. B. Paisley

CATALOGUE OF
THE PAISLEY COLLECTION

27 TRACTION ENGINES & ROAD ROLLERS
400 LOCOMOTIVE & TRACTION PLATES
Locomotive Splasher Plates, Smoke Box Door Rings,
Stationary Engines & Pumps, Engine Lamps,
Threshing Drums & Other Tackle, 1914/18 German
Field Gun, 180 Volts. of 'The Engineer' and
'Engineering' from 1857, etc., etc.

FOR SALE BY PUBLIC AUCTION
at MANOR FARM, HOLYWELL, Nr. ST. IVES, CAMBS.

WEDNESDAY 1 OCTOBER 1980 at 10.30 a.m. precisely
Traction Engines, etc., at 2.00 p.m.

ON VIEW   30 September 10.30 a.m.
to 4.00 p.m. and evening of sale.
Licensed Bar and Refreshments

The Paisley collection sale catalogue 1.10.1980

Tom Paisley farmed the 534-acre Manor Farm for more than 30 years, until his death in 1980, during which time Holywell was a mecca for steam enthusiasts

Old Timers! Jack Barter (1894-1988) with 'Sampson' (1901-), an Aveling and Porter type LC8 Engine, which started life in Chatham Docks. It later became a showman's locomotive. W. Stearn: 'a real man's engine'

Holywell strawberry fields 1954

Mr O Skinner inspects
his fine crop of Climax
strawberries

Mr Skinner's maiden plantation being
inspected by Horticultural Field Officer

Gerald Baily inspects an
average size 'Climax'

A fruit gatherer at work: small on the left, large on the right - tricky!

David Tabbitt weighing up the fruit in 2lb
chip baskets - six to a tray

Whole families could be engaged on seasonal work. It
was all go, dawn till dusk, six or seven days a week

High Street, Needingworth

Pound Hill, beginning of Needingworth village. The house on the left has been demolished to make way for new dwellings

Horse and trap outside The Priory

The Rose and Crown Public House Now 'Crossways', a private house, sometime antique shop

'Crossways'
The only thatched house in Needingworth

The Old Baptist Chapel front and next the house of Wilf Senescall and the baker's shop of his brother Stan

Needingworth High Street with Chris Bedford's shop and post office to the right. The woman in the bonnet facing a doorway is unknown

The village fire hooks hang on the wall of Sandifers barn. They are used for pulling off the thatched roofs of cottages which have caught fire.

The Hammer and Anvil Public House, now 53 High Street, and next door at No 55, the Wheatsheaf - the home of Cecil Prior, the Village Crier

The Red Bull Public House was opposite Silver Lane. The Chestnuts is on the right of the road leading out of the village towards Bluntisham

Another view of the Red Bull with Oliver Peters at the door

The Three Horseshoes (*far left*), the
Chestnuts (*centre right*) (built
around 1710) and old farm buildings

The White Horse Public House, 7 High Street,
Needingworth. William Stringer (landlord
1920/30s). Now the Fish Farm

The Three Horseshoes Public House opposite the Chestnuts with Bill Mason on the cart

The Queens Head Public House - now the only remaining public house open in the village

A pair of cottages opposite Daintree Farm, also now long gone. Charlie Sutton, chimney sweep and carpenter, lived in one of them

A pair of thatched cottages next to Daintree Farm. Jimmy Raven lived in one of them

Needingworth Church Street: fruit farming and the Asplins

The southern aspect of the land rising from the Ouse Valley is ideal for the fruit farmer. In the 19th to 20th century thousands of tons of fruit were gathered and sent by rail to the canning and jam-making factories. Carriage-loads of strawberries, gooseberries, apples and plums were despatched to London and the midland towns. In 1912 the Asplin family, already established at Over, migrated to begin fruit farming on the Needingworth slopes. Leonard Asplin, pictured with the weighing machine, was the first to cross the river. His brother Russell followed in 1919.

Leonard Asplin with weighing machine

An early picture of Russell (1890-1933) with strawberry pickers

Willie Gaunt with his daughter Kathy take a break from shopkeeping to admire Wilfred Asplin (b.29.7.1921) in his perambulator, while Louisa Asplin looks on from the shop doorway

Apple gatherers at Wesley Farm pause for the cameraman. Stan and Wilf Asplin with George Easton and unnamed ladies

Leonard Asplin in trilby hat and his gang of plum pickers

The child nursing her doll is Mary Gilkes who grew up to marry Wilfred on 1.10.1949

Believed to be the first reaping machine in
Needingworth - replacing the scythe and sickle

Overcote Lane, Needingworth
Asplin horses 'Punch' and 'Judy'
in the hayfield c.1930
Bob Parish's house far left

Overcote Lane, Needingworth 2004
Needingworth Bowls Club, the same field
Bob Parish's house left of centre

Cyril Asplin (1911-1988) was organist at the Methodist Church, St Ives, for 60 years and had a lifetime love of organ music. In his music room, seating 250, he gave many concerts for charitable causes. He also travelled up and down the country playing his Hammond and Lowry organs for Cheshire homes, Over-60s clubs and disabled groups etc., ably supported by his second wife, Valerie. Cyril's father, Leonard, was organist for many years at Needingworth Baptist Chapel

Cyril Asplin was both fruit farmer and businessman. In the early days of commercial refrigeration he converted the old maltings in Church Street to cold storage for the Ministry of Food and for Chivers. Here he is pictured with his new tractor

Church Street, Needingworth

No. 4   High Street, Needingworth

Beyond the cattle watering in the pond is 'The Willows', a row of three cottages at the time of this photograph

The signpost points to Holywell one mile along Church Street.
The brick building on the left was erected by William Martin Thorp whose initials in ironwork may still be seen on the gable end. This was the butcher's shop.

After the storm – reflections in the swollen pond

Ducks on the village pond. 'Bakers Dozen' on the right. Godfrey the baker delivered by pony and cart. After Godfrey a fish and chip shop opened c.1930 and served through the window by the road

Another view of Church Street. No pavements and doorsteps – just above flood level

Hawkes Lane, Needingworth, looking from the pond left to the High Street 1936

Leslie Harvey. Field milking 1960s with Nigel in the pick-up

Rhoda Mary Harvey (née Sandifer) with her sons Brian and Leslie. The black cow 'Royal Oak' weighed 16½ cwt

A pair of steam traction engines making their way through the village. Spot Nigel Harvey's head! The pond has been filled in and is now grass with a seat for weary travellers

1903 The village school
with Headmaster Arthur
Rowland and his wife, the
Headmistress

Holywell School, early 1920s
Back row boys from left: W Cooper, O Norman, Roy Sandifer, Cliff Cooper, ? O'Dell,
Charles ?, Sam Coulson, Reg Smith
Back row middle from left: Mamie Hayes, Gladys Ballard, Eric Tabbitt, Les Norman,
Arthur Howlett, Reg Wilmer, Sid Tabbitt, Cyril White, Frank Tabbitt, Mr Kirby
Middle row from left: Edith O'Dell, Maud Dobson, Eileen Blewitt,
Winnie Goodge, Murial Mansfield, Betty Ibbett, Mabel Tabbitt, Mary Edwards
Front row from left: Muriel Armstrong, Margaret Childs,
Amy Coulson, Muriel Prior, Ida Benton

School photograph c.1925 (some pupils are unidentified)
Back row boys from left: Reg Smith, Cyril White, Arthur Howlett, Frank
Tabbitt, George Stringer, Reg Tabbitt, Sam Coulson
Row of girls from left: Ida Benton, Muriel Armstrong, Edith O'Dell, —, Eileen
Blewitt, Eleanor Few, Betty Ibbett, —, —, Margaret Childs
Middle row girls: ? Skinner, —, Olive Parr, —, Violet Dodson, Muriel Prior
Front row boys: Eric Tabbitt, Walter Tabbitt, —, —, –, Leslie Harvey

Holywell Village School – building now demolished

Row of old cottages demolished to make
way for Harris Crescent. Mrs Papworth
chatting with Mrs Vawser, a visitor

Thatched cottages opposite Park View looking toward the pond

Mabel Wright 'Mavis' came with her grandfather, parents and four siblings to live at Mill Cottage (rent 2/- (10p) per week) on his retirement from the Metropolitan Police. The children attended the village school and eventually the family moved to Mafeking House.

   Mavis' exciting life and lonely death are described in the book *Beautiful and Beloved* by her son Tristan de vere Cole

Wartime. Mavis pictured in women's Land Army days

1909 Holywell Post Mill and Mill Cottage

The mill, owned by Fred Harvey, was last used to grind cattle feed by Stanley Senescall in 1911. It fell into gradual disrepair and finally collapsed in a storm one night in 1940. The grindstones crashed into the wall of Joan Papworth's bedroom and rendered her petrified and unable to speak for several hours

This sketch shows the brick-built roundhouse which was used to store grain or flour awaiting collection after the harvest gleanings

War Memorial, Needingworth

Private George Lantaff (1911-1945) joined the Northants Territorials and was 'called-up' at the out-break of war in 1939. He died on 8th January 1945 in Burma from a sniper's bullet. Lantaff's name is not on the village memorial but is inscribed on the St Ives Cross of Sacrifice and on the memorial in Holywell church

The war memorial and lock-up looking east

George's widow, Mabel Lantaff née Tabbitt (15.4.1912-), was born and is still living in the vil-lage. She has two married daughters, Faith Hamilton and Marian Neave.

High Street/Overcote Lane junction. Before the erection of the war memorial a pony-driven children's roundabout stood here on the grass triangle during the vil-lage feast – the ride cost a penny a time

Feeding an inmate with beer through a straw

The parish memorial is in the form of a Portland stone obelisk unveiled in December 1920 and paid for by public subscription

The lock-up in Needingworth is a small brick building with a wooden door and barred window. A stone plaque over the door reads 'Built 1858'. There are half-torn posters on the front and a boy and girl leaning against the building. On the back of this picture was written 'The boy was a Sandifer'

War Memorial with Jack Butcher's farmhouse (now demolished) in the background

The Sandifers of Needingworth

For five generations spanning three centuries, the Sandifers farmed the fields around Needingworth and had a major influence on the lives of the villagers by marriage and employment.

William, born in 1796, fathered Robert (1824-1881) – he had four wives and 14 children between them. Robert's son Alfred (1856-1927) had 15 children with his wife who outlived him by 20 years. Alfred's third son, William D. Sandifer (1880-1962) had three sons who were the last of the family to farm in Needingworth

Sandifers produced their own brand of cream cheese which became popular in the early Edwardian era and was marketed under the 'Needona' label. It had a regular outlet with Crowsons of London and on at least one occasion Crowson's employees were brought to Needingworth by charabanc for entertainment at Priory Farm. Isaac Crowson lived at Victoria House, Needingworth.

SOLE MAKERS OF
"NEEDONA" (REGD. BRAND)
CREAM CHEESE AND
OTHER DAIRY PRODUCTS

Awarded Certificate in County Clean Milk Competition

W. D. Sandifer & Son

Needona Dairies
BRIDGE STREET
ST. IVES, HUNTS.

FARMS AT NEEDINGWORTH

Above: the Sandifers business card

Left: Victoria House, Needingworth

The Priory, Needingworth, c.1924
Left to right: Harry Sandifer at the head of Kitty the pony with
Alfred and Mary Jane in the trap with three of their children

West view of the Priory

A family portrait of Alfred Sandifer (1856-1927) and his wife Mary Jane
(1858-1947). Fifteen of their children survived to adulthood

Front
view of
the
Priory

Images of
a village

___Chestnuts Farm, Needingworth

The Chestnuts, built around 1710, was a busy working farm. The scenes that follow show the Women's Land Army girls at work and various views of haymaking, harvesting and dairying between 1930 and 1932.

May Edwards and Arthur Howlett

Harvesters

Jack Seekings

Hay picnic in West Fen 1932

Loading hay, Chestnut Farm 1932

Les Roofe with bucket
and stool ready for
milking 1938

Wesleyan Methodism

In 1846 the Rev McGee, Rector of the parish, was concerned that there had never been a school in the village. His plans to build a school failed but he did buy the Wesleyan Chapel which had fallen into disuse. In 1875 the village school along Holywell Road was built and once again the old chapel was unused - the Sandifer family took it over as a grain store. In more recent days it became the village youth club until finally it was demolished and the site taken into the Baptist car park. The Gazeteer and Directory of the County of Huntingdon 1854 under Needingworth states 'There is a school here for small children, supported by the Rector'. This is believed to be it.

The new Wesleyan chapel was built in 1888 at a cost of £262. It, too, succumbed to the passage of time and closed in 1972 to be converted into a private residence

The old Wesleyan Chapel (looking west)
(The Weekly Gazette of 10th September 1847 reported in its list of properties etc destroyed in the great fire that '. . . the Wesleyan Chapel scorched and injured').

The old Wesleyan Chapel with the village store and post office by the telegraph pole (looking east)

Older residents have many happy memories of the Wesleyan Chapel and those who served its cause. This is the only known picture of the Sunday School c.1946 taken opposite the chapel where a house now stands

The Baptists

The Particular Baptist Chapel was formed on 13th March 1767 and the Meeting House built on what is now the cemetery in Meeting Lane. The congregation grew and a new chapel was erected on a site in the High Street in 1861.

On 6th January 1928 a devastating storm swept the country causing great damage and the roof of the chapel lifted and was left in ruins.

Great damage was done to the interior and the organ was destroyed

The destruction was so serious that the building was pulled down and a New Providence Chapel erected and consecrated on 9th August 1928.

New Providence Chapel erected in 1928

Dorothy Sandifer being escorted by her father Alfred
Sandifer (1856-1927), to her marriage to George Pelham
at the Baptist Chapel

Parson Saunders resident 1913-1940 with
his wife and donkey-drawn buggy

Pike & Eel and the Meridian

In the 1920s Sid Broughton was landlord and farmer and operated the ferry which, before the age of the motor car, was much used as a 'shortcut' to Over and Cambridge.

The Pike and Eel at Overcote was in earlier times a private residence known as Over Court. At one time Colonel Hampden, a cousin of Oliver Cromwell, lived here

Cromwell is said to have planned some of his campaigns here

Norah Tabbitt, Schoolteacher at Over, used the ferry daily, cycling to and from school to her home at Holywell. With the coming of the motor car, the ferry gradually ceased to be used and in the late 1930s only a large flat-bottomed punt was available for cyclists at sixpence (2½p) each crossing.

The Pike and Eel is known to locals as 'The Pike'.

The Over carrier Bismark Norman pictured here, had regular pick-up points and passengers between Over and St Ives. His van had many compartments for poultry, piglets, eggs and fruit, etc.

Clare Burgess, standing by the riverside Pike and Eel sign, is now Mrs Clare Barker and teaches at Holywell School

The author's grandparents regularly travelled between
Cambridge and Warboys using the ferry except in the
severest of flood conditions, thereby saving at least
seven miles journey each way

The Pike and Eel 2004

Further views of the Pike and
Eel and the Ferry

St Ives, Overcote the Ferry

OVERCOTE FERRY HUNTS

A stone marking the Greenwich meridian on the footpath beside the Ouse: an upright oblong of grey stone with a vertical line down the middle, with 'Greenwich Meridian Line' carved on it, so arranged that the line forms the letter 'I' in each word.

Located on the left-hand river bank path between the Pike and Eel and Brownshill Staunch.

Needingworth Level Crossing, Gifford's Farm, Chicory Factory

The gatekeeper's cottage at the Needingworth level crossing. The gates were frequently
smashed by an oncoming train because they had not been closed to road traffic

Compass Point industrial estate now occupies the site of the English Chicory Factory – formerly a brickworks. The Brickmakers Arms Public House and its successor, 'Tunari' (home of Teddy Ilott, Chicory Factory Manager), were both demolished as the site was redeveloped.

'Tunari'

Experimental crops of the chicory root were grown at Holywell to produce the kiln-dried chicory for use in coffee products. In the beginning Belgian workers were brought over for their expertise in managing the kilns.

The Chicory Factory in Needingworth Road, St Ives. A tall brick-built structure with doorways and windows on three storeys and complicated brick structures on the roof, with a curved-top pediment with the word 'Chicory Ltd'. In the foreground, under construction, are linear structures of thick timber, possibly to do with the building but may be to hold dumps of chicory?

Dockey time for this cheerful gang of apple gatherers working at
Chivers, Gifford's Farm, Needingworth, c.1950

Social events

Probably Feast Week, decorated
pram competition

'Vote Liberal' 1925
Organising commitee and helpers

Holywell-cum-Needingworth Flower Show - award of cups and trophies
Left to right: Kathy Cooper, 'Guest', Mrs Musson, Maud Papworth, Jack Davidson, John Baily, Florrie Dellar, George Knight

Jack Arnold from Holywell (on left), and Charlie Stocker from Needingworth - friendly rivals and stalwart competitors over many years at the annual Village Flower and Vegetable Show

Women's Institute (c.1948)

Picture includes:

Back row: Mrs Norman, Mrs Millie Morgan, Mrs Peters, Mrs Prior, (next two not known), Mrs Benton, (next not known), Mrs Mabel Sutton, Mrs Dorothy Butcher, (next not known), Mrs Joan Jordan, Mrs Darby, Mrs Coulson, Mrs Legg, Mrs Blakesley Jnr, Mrs Jean Bailey

Front row: Mrs Shannon, Mrs Cook, (next not known), Mrs Broakes, Mrs Pearce Higgins, (next not known), Mrs Dorothy Barret, Joy Legg, Mrs Thaxter, Mrs Blakesley, Mrs Lissamore

Guides and Brownies (1961)

Back left to right: Mrs Howes, Anne Howes, Freda Blewitt, Ruth Henson, Susan Davidson, Jean Tabbitt, Susan Tabbitt, Jennifer Cooper, Ann Hunter, Sarah McPherson, Judy Copping

Front left to right: Kay Cook, Valerie Tabbitt, Penny Davidson, Barbara Howes, Margaret McGlade, Joan Morgan, Carol Gray, Sandra Barson, Yvonne Wilson, Alison Sandifer, Pat Irwin, Mary Tabbitt

The village sign which stands on Pound Hill was presented to the parish by the Women's Institute in 1996 to mark their 75th anniversary.

Michael Williamson is seen receiving the sign from Valery Norman, President of Holywell-cum-Needingworth Women's Institute with members of the WI and Parish Councillors witnessing the event

1995 Prime Minister John Major opens Needingworth bypass

The Women's Institute meeting at the Village School. At last they have a cupboard of their very own!

Back row from left: Mrs Sutton, Mrs Norman, Mrs Peters, Mrs Darby, Mrs Wrigley

Front row left: Mrs Barrat, Mrs Thaxter, Mrs Butcher, Mrs Benton

Front row right: Mrs Legg, Mrs Jordan (Joan Butcher), Mrs Stocker, Mrs Bedford

Golden Jubilee
June 2002

Celebration tea, Needingworth High Street, 1945

Village characters

Villages breed characters and Cecil Prior well filled the role at Needingworth. The 1930s were his heyday - as self-appointed village crier, he would don his top hat and morning coat, mount his cycle and, with the aid of his bell, shout news of national and local urgency from vantage points established by tradition.

His everyday occupation of fruit agent and smallholder, coupled with a milk round, dillydallying and seasonal pressures, led to him being nicknamed 'the midnight milkman'. His customers were never quite sure to which day their delivery belonged!

Cecil Prior. Village Crier; milkman; smallholder; agent for fruit wholesalers; extrovert natural entertainer; always 'catching up'; 'Midnight milkman'

Shadrach Smith 'Old Shady'

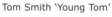
Tom Smith 'Young Tom'

The Smith family of gypsies came from 'out Bedford way' and settled in a field off Needingworth Road, St Ives. The family consisted of Shadrack, his wife, sons Tom and Bob, and their daughter Belinda. They lived in igloo-like constructions made from young willow poles and covered in bits of tarpaulin or anything that would keep out the rain. Belinda had her own igloo and the boys slept together.

They cooked on an open fire and drew water from a well in the hedgerow. As they went about seasonal work on the farms, a piebald pony was harnessed to their trolley and a lurcher ran beneath. Fruit-picking, sugar beet singling or lifting all came their way. Off season Shadrack made willow pegs and 'the old lady' sold them, along with lace and ribbon, door to door.

Lifting beet
Painting by J. E. R. Godderidge

Sport

Sid Brown signs the land agreement with the Parish Council, witnessed by Jack Arnold and Brian Webster in 1987: founder members of the first Bowls Club in Needingworth. The Club flourishes with six rinks and 90 members

An early photograph of a Needingworth football team. Clearly seen is the leather-clad football which needed regular treatment with dubbin water repellant

A 1920s cup-winning team. Seated on the right hand is Jimmy Hodkinson and behind him is Captain Edwards. Bare headed at the left of the back row is Wilf Senescall

The Needingworth side of 1933–34
Back row left to right: Captain Edwards, C Cooper, T Marriott, W White, S Pyett, L Marriott, L Simons, W Mason
Front row: G Coulson, R Tabbitt, S Tabbitt, E Tabbitt, L Norman

The 1947–48 team
Back row left to right: Mr Aubrey, O Norman, A White, H White, A Blakesly, R Smith, A Howlett, J Dicks, Mr Robinson, S Peacock
Front row: E Tabbitt, J Parr, C Read, R Davis, K Sandifer, D Millington

Images of
a village

Nineteenth century public houses in Holywell and Needingworth

The White Horse
The Hammer and Anvil
The Three Horseshoes
The George

The Rose and Crown
The Lion and the Lamb
The Ducks Nest
The Red Bull
The Brother Struggler

The Queens Head
The Wheatsheaf
The Brickmakers Arms
The Carpenters Arms

The Anchor

The Ferryboat

The White Horse

The Pike and Eel

FINIS